© 2023 Experiments in Fiction

Kim M. Russell
All Grown Up Now
All rights reserved. No part of this publication may be reproduced, stored in a retrieval system or transmitted in any form or by any means, electronic, mechanical, photocopying, recording or otherwise without the prior permission of the publisher or in accordance with the provisions of the Copyright, Designs and Patents Act 1988 or under the terms of any licence permitting limited copying issued by the Copyright Licensing Agency.

Published by: Experiments in Fiction

Cover photographs: Courtesy of the Author

Cover Design by: Experiments in Fiction

ISBN: 978-1-7394044-3-7

Kim M. Russell

ALL GROWN UP NOW

All Grown Up Now

KIM M. RUSSELL

Contents

Beginnings	9
Scarf Magic	11
Washing Day	12
Ironing	13
Making Pastry	14
The Widowed Aunts	15
The Landing at the Top of the Stairs	16
In the Garden	18
Night of Sparks	19
Necklace	20
A South London Childhood	21
Magnificent for a Moment	22
Are We There Yet?	23
Midsummer Verges	24
The Proust Effect	25
Back to School	27
Up-Ended	28
Becoming a She-Wolf	29
Fragile Bond of Sisterhood	30
Newgrange	31
Sonnet on the Marriage of my Only Daughter	32
Wedding Dress	33
To My Unborn Grandchild	34
Coty	35
Self-Portrait with Hands	36

On the Anniversary of My Mother's Death	37
Only Our Last Conversation Remains	38
Poetic Voice	39
To the young poet of the future	40
About The Author	41

In memory of Nan and Grandad.

— *Kim M. Russell*

Beginnings

I see myself in photographs,
a baby in a plastic bath,
a solitary fair-haired child
swinging on a garden gate,
skipping up the tiled path
of a post-war terrace,
tiptoeing up
a carmine step
in my blue duffle coat.

There were hot summers,
counting earwigs in the pebbledash,
picking purple weeds that gave me a rash.
There was the scullery,
the constant smell of gas
and tea towels boiling in a soapy pan,
and the noisy siren from the wireworks;
I picked out the copper bits
from the soles of Granddad's boots.

KIM M. RUSSELL

There were Sunday mornings,
hiding under the feather bedspread
and jumping down the stairs,
and Sunday afternoons
watching movies on the telly,
tap-dancing on the lino
like Ginger Rogers and Fred Astaire,
and ice cream from the chiming van
to make a cream soda float.

Scarf Magic

My grandmother never went out without a headscarf.
She had plenty, all neatly folded on a shelf in a low cupboard,
within easy reach.

They were mostly chiffon, rainbows
demanding to be unfolded and swirled in the air
like fairy wings.

Opened to full capacity, they seemed enormous,
perfect for dressing up
or parachutes.

At the bottom was her footwear.
She never complained about the pile
of shoes and slippers,

or the crumpled fairy wings that floated in the air.
She always applauded singing, dancing,
and scarf magic.

Washing Day

I smell soap bubbles in the scullery,
steamy clean and floating through my early
years; my grandmother's hands red and hot,
tea-towels boiling in the biggest pot
as I turn the handle of the wringer,
reminded always to 'Mind your finger!'

I sit on the back step
while she raises the line with a wooden prop:
bath towels and sheets flap above the trees,
vests and shirts dance in the breeze,
and I inhale the scent of fresh linen.

Later, when the washing is dry,
I help collect the pegs and fold the sheets
ready for ironing. It's a treat
to climb into a newly made bed
and lay down my buzzing head
on a washing day scented pillow,
one that I'd seen billow,
and drift slowly
into soap bubble dreams.

Ironing

It's a wet Tuesday, rain
spits at the curtained window
and I'm listening to the radio,
following in Grandmother's footsteps.
The iron steams. Clothes rescued
from the line are scented
with raindrops, creased
and pleading to be smoothed.
I press fabric between iron and board,
breathe in warm memories
and slip down the years
to the lily-of-the-valley embrace
of the woman who taught me
how to iron away a rainy day.

Making Pastry

I remember the intimacy
of warm-kitchen days, when hands
touched over a huge bowl or fingers
gripped together round a wooden spoon
in snowstorms of flour and avalanches
of butter, eggs and sugar, both tied
up in aprons, red-cheeked and bright-eyed,
mixing and stirring, baking and burning
pies and tarts to tempt and delight
Granddad when he came home.
I didn't touch a crumb
because Nanny made a special
sugar-and-butter-filled pastry just for me,
my own baking-day delicacy.

The Widowed Aunts

As a young child, I would often visit
my three widowed great-great-aunts,
who sipped tea and nibbled biscuits
between unpicking news and gossip.

In the twilight of a backstairs kitchen,
I was a child, to be seen and not heard,
listening to tales of the distant and long-dead,
tapping patent pumps on a table leg.

Those wizened women, drenched in mothballs,
whose knowing eyes had seen two wars,
were proud of the black weeds they wore,
spot-cleaned and rubbed into shiny patches.

They were unaware I thought them witches,
weaving a spell of violet and lavender,
or the overpowering cut of camphor
that made me cough and hold my breath.

It seemed they wore the scent of death
and yet, sitting around the tuneless upright,
those waxy widows beamed with light
as they trilled Victorian parlour songs
and cheeky ditties from the music hall -
my aunts weren't witches after all.

The Landing at the Top of the Stairs

My five year old self sits on the toilet,
door open so I can see the top flight
of stairs inhabited by shadows from a skylight.
There's a closed door at the end of the twilight;
escaping from the keyless lock is sunlight
full of dust motes that float.

I am torn between a monster
in the plumbing that I know is coming
and the unknown behind the door.
I've never pulled the chain before,
believing that the water's roar
would rouse the ghost in the room.

In winter, the bathroom has an icy chill
and the added terror of a paraffin heater,
its overwhelming stink and the wavy thrill
of heat warning the bogeyman to stay
away. And then one day,
the door is open, its secrets spilled:

a broken chair, worn cushions, a battered
suitcase full of old lady's tattered
underwear, pinafores and canvas shoes -
remnants of the wizened ghost
we'd visit every Sunday afternoon,
shut up in a different kind of room -

my great grandmother, locked in her head
with her own ghosts, lost and demented.

In the Garden

Confined to house and wireworks walls,
he was a caged animal picking tiny nuggets
of copper from boot soles like thorns from paws.

On weekdays, at one for dinner and five
for tea, deep in the fabric of his work clothes
and his very being, he carried home
the metallic tang of blood and sweat.

A victim of the Blitz, shaky hands and sleepless
nights betrayed the calm of face and voice.

But in the garden, sun on his back
and a tuneful whistle on peppermint breath,
reciting their names like holy prayers,
he taught me to dead-head peony and rose,
and sprinkle the dry earth with can and hose.

Night of Sparks

I remember
my first fifth of November:
I was five,
bundled up in coat,
knitted gloves, scarf and hat,
breathing smoke and stars,
a fizzing sparkler in my hand,
spellbound by the Catherine wheel
spinning embers on the garden fence -
it cost Granddad sixpence.

Necklace

An old-fashioned red London bus
takes me back to childhood's
sleepy night-ride home
from my grandparents' house:
tucked between Mum and Dad,
bare legs on fuzzy seat,
folding concertinas of paper tickets,
hypnotised by the perfume of exhaust,
rumble of engine, and the window's
black and empty gaze. I believed
the stars – obscured by sulphurous
streetlights – had been caught,
strung in a sparkly dance
of headlights in the distance.

A South London Childhood

Balconies and concrete stairs,
beery piss in broken lifts,
every night the same old prayers,
someone get us out of here.

Tightrope walking on the fence,
leap the gap between the sheds,
long walk to the traffic lights,
sideswiped by a motorbike.

Buttercups and dandelions
crowd long grass by rusty gates;
in the alley, shadows fall
where the friendly flasher waits.

Magnificent for a Moment

You spent years underground,
a larva, your skin brittle
and papery. Vulnerable,
you built your cocoon in darkness
as black as your carapace.

I found you that day,
a jet flash in the May sun
basking in the heat
of urban concrete.

I admired your gloss
and spectacular size,
a stag among beetles
ready to lock antler jaws
in a bristling wrestle for a mate.

But I only caught a glimpse
of chestnut wings
as you flew off
into the London sunset.

Are We There Yet?

it's just a glint
from the brow of a hill
like the blue stroke
of a fountain pen

and then the coach stops
and you breathe in
a quirky whiff of damp dog
that tickles your nose

and your ears fill
with the crash of waves
that fizz around your fears
with a gasp of goose bumps

it creases like a screwed-up paper bag
tips the horizon on its axis
a twisting kaleidoscope of senses
dreams trickling through sandy hands

Midsummer Verges

Content in our garden's leafy shade,
I think back to weedy margins
on a distant council estate,
full of dandelions and significance,

between pan-hot pavement
and simmering black tar,
a strip of withered grass,
litter-strewn and dotted with dog mess,

where bike wheels used to spin, click, tick,
where kids clutched coins in sweaty hands
at Mr Whippy's ice cream van,
and we found our first four leaf clover.

The summers of childhood are long over,
blown away like gossamer seeds,
and I sit here at sunset, taking stock,
puffing away at a dandelion clock.

The Proust Effect

I inhale
the summer trail
of dust and flowers
where we played for hours
sniffing wild fennel studded with snails

on the way to school
wrapped in scarves
of damp autumn fog
we dodge the acridity of dog
turds and the putrid decay
of rubbish in the alley

greeted by the school canteen
with its pungency
of cabbage and custard

and later home
where Grandmother's lily
echoes in the valley
of childhood
her kitchen steeped
in a gauze of gas
washing powder
warm pastry and ironing

Granddad's coat
fresh from the factory
reeks of metal and biscuit
dunked in workman's tea

olfactory instruments
perform an aromatic aria
in a landscape of smells
and my nose for nostalgia

Back to School

In the first week of childhood's September,
going back to school was surreal
and I discovered a new sense of smell:
new uniform, shoes and plimsolls,
and the scent of sharpened pencils in satchels.

I breathed in stale lost property masked with polish
from parquet floors of classrooms and the hall;
chalk-free blackboards and bare pastel walls;
blank exercise books and lined paper in reams,
waiting for fresh ink, essays and poems.

I sniffed pungent autumn in the air,
the promise of leaves and conkers everywhere,
the early creeping in of tea-time and gloam,
when cocoa and buttered crumpets steamed
on the kitchen table when we got home.

Up-Ended

I miss the freedom
of childhood summers
threading daisies
searching for four-leaf clover
turning an upside
down handstand
against the wall
dresses tucked in knickers
laughing at each other's
frown
that was an up-ended
smile
we're all grown up now

Becoming a She-Wolf

The crepuscular dawn
of teenage-hood, tainted
with the tang of menses moon,
invokes a howl of hair
in places unexplored
as yet.

Nobody told me about the free-
fall
or the strange sweetness
of explosions in the darkness,
lit only by the wolfish teeth
of an alpha smile.

Fragile Bond of Sisterhood

Open oceans cannot stop these tides
of grief, the trickle and splash of sorrow
over-spilling rivers, bursting through sides
of lakes with the constant ebb and flow,
deceived by the duplicity of a cancerous
two-faced moon. I believed that blood
was thicker but you turned hazardous
and you broke the fragile bond of sisterhood.

The density of water, particularly the salty kind,
allows me to float on the surface of my grief,
washing the guilt away, clearing my murky mind,
only my heart is still tossed like a leaf.

Newgrange

When I took you to a bend
in the Boyne and a monument older than Stonehenge,
you were brand new.

Walking round the mound,
I counted out a nursery rhyme of kerbstones
guarding ancient bones.

We entered the gloom,
followed a passage to the single tomb, at solstice
when shadows are pierced

by a shaft of sunlight
where ancestors were buried in a stone edifice,
and past and present come together.

Sonnet on the Marriage of my Only Daughter

In the coldness of a November night,
when the full moon shone with silvery light,
I gave birth to a fairy foundling girl
of violet eyes and finely-spun gold curls.
She tugged at my heart on her first day at school,
unravelled my soul on a spinning spool,
a sea nymph building castles on the shore,
a petulant teen trouncing out the door,
put tears in my eyes when she left our home,
eager to have adventures of her own.
Now someone else loves her as much as I,
who wants to keep her safe and make her smile.
I can still see her giggling on a swing;
he only gets a glimpse of my changeling

Wedding Dress

     In a champagne froth of lace,
          embroidered intricacy and pearl drops,
I barely recognise your face.

You were once a changeling with violet eyes
          and happier in cotton than in lace.
     I remember stanching your childhood teardrops

     and now, I blot my own equivocal drops.
You are a joyful bride,
     blooming in your layers of lace.

I watch your ringed fingers interlace as one last tear
drops,
     daughter.

To My Unborn Grandchild

Dearest little one,
I am counting down the days
and knitting. I am amazed
at the butterflies of anticipation,
imagining your eyes, mouth and nose,
your tiny fingers and toes,
the fresh-baked smell from the top
of your head. I can't wait to sing
the songs I once sang to your mother,
and the ones mine once sang to me.
I have so many stories to tell
and poems to read to you until
your eyelashes flutter and I will keep
watch as you drift off to sleep.

Coty

It comes to me
through autumn smoke,
the burning of damp leaves,
that pricks the eyes
and chokes the breath,
the funeral pall of summer's death –
a hint of you drifts through the trees,
teasing on the goose-bump breeze
the scent of Coty powder on your face,
always just a trace
of you in me.

Self-Portrait with Hands

They have teased music from a classical guitar,
woven brightly dyed wool into a winter knit,
and pencilled themselves into a sketch.
They cover my face now, as I pose
before a speckled, frameless mirror
tucked away, out of sight, under the stairs.
She's there, somewhere in the shadows,
the one whose fingers plucked and drew -
how did they stiffen into wrinkled claws?
I move my hands, reveal my mother's face,
time-stamped with crow's feet and a trace
of the sparkle of her timeless, girlish smile.

On the Anniversary of My Mother's Death

Like the sky maps sketched
on the bird brains of the geese
flying overhead this morning
in their flocks and vees,
her gentle face is etched
into my genealogy.
I hear their honk and chatter
loud and clear, flying by
as if it doesn't matter
that a day cannot be erased
by hoar frost. Yes, it's here again,
sparkling just like all those years ago,
stiffening remaining leaves and
silvering the grass outside my window.

Only Our Last Conversation Remains

Virus-like in their determination,
years mutate and, before we know it,
all that remains is our last conversation,
hanging in the air like a reverberation

from a bass guitar – a note
that will eventually end.

Each of us had our perspective,
a handful of photographs, faded letters
and postcards the only proof of our mutual past,
of the love and trust we thought would last

forever - until we eventually
grew apart my friend.

That is my reason for writing these lines,
these inky tattoos, outpourings of love,
this quiet strumming of nostalgic thoughts
growing into a last conversation
of sorts, a conversation, my friend,
that must definitely come to an end.

Poetic Voice

I yell into the depths of night
and dawn has never seemed so far away.
Among shadows loiter nightmares,
immeasurable moments of black despair,

but it only takes a single moonbeam
and, like owls and foxes, words appear,
hooting and barking until it seems
that they are cavorting in the light.

Hypnos still presses heavy on this poet's eyes;
nevertheless I am roused from my bed
by the St Vitus dance of poems in my head,
urging me to leave the comfort of the covers,

take one sleepy pigeon step after another
through the darkness and write them down instead.

To the young poet of the future

I picture you gazing at a star,
concerned that you are still so far
from becoming the poet
that you wish to be.

From my position of retrospection,
I promise that your journey is the best lesson:
you will be buffeted by storms and squalls,
fluctuations in the weather of the soul,

soothed by sunny days and gentle breezes,
fuelling emotions that will swell and fill
you to the brim, then drip and spill
from heart and soul to pen to pool

into elegies, odes and sonnets,
the harvest of your poetic climate.

About The Author

Kim M. Russell has been writing poetry since she was very young; she has written every day since she retired from teaching, blogging at writinginnorthnorfolk.com and hosting at the dVerse Poets Pub. Her poems have been published on-line by Visual Verse, Spillwords, The Ekphrastic Review, Pure Haiku and Poetry Pea, and in printed anthologies: Afflatus Magazine, *Chiaroscuro, Darkness and Light* (a dVerse Anthology), *Anthology of Aunts* and *Second Place Rosette* (The Emma Press), *Peeking Cat, Fieldwork* (New Nature Writing from East Anglia), the *Poetry Pea Journals, The Anthropocene Hymnal, Wounds I Healed* (Experiments in Fiction), and *Dark Confessions* (Black Bough Poetry), as well as a piece of flash fiction in *Flash, I love you!* (Paper Swans Press). Kim has self-published *Between Heartbeats*, an anthology of short fiction, and a novel for children, *Joe and Nelly*. She lives in Norfolk with her husband and two cats.

Also Available from EIF

Archery in the UK
by Nick Reeves and Ingrid Wilson

ISBN: 9781739757786

Inspired by the *Lyrical Ballads* of Wordsworth and Coleridge, two authors set out to pen a contemporary homage to this timeless collection. As the collaboration progresses, however, the poetry and the unique narrative it carries takes on a life of its own. Thus, the authors come to tell their story through a collection of ballads, sonnets, pantoums and other forms.

In The Shadow of Rainbows
by Selma Martin

ISBN: 9781739404444

In this dazzling debut poetry collection of over 60 carefully selected poems, author Selma Martin points the way to the beauty in the everyday, the shadow of the rainbow, and the silver lining at the edge of every cloud.

Favouring lyrical forms, and revelling in rhymes and musical language, the individual poems in this collection harmonise together in symphonic splendour to form an enlightening and delightful whole.

40 Poems At 40
by Ingrid Wilson

ISBN: 9781739757700

40 Poems is the debut poetry collection from Ingrid Wilson. It is poetry of place and space, and here lie the clues and the beauty to Wilson's poetry. Her work is charted, landscaped, travelled, explorative and laden with adventure. There are bright, sad, dreamy postcards telling of the beauty of Barcelona, the slate-grey, but singing, county of Cumbria, Malaga, 'the emptiness' of Manchester, 'the fields' of London, 'the ancient pasts' of Newcastle, the mysterious beauty of Slovenia, Venice and its lullaby… lapping water is never far from her ear.

Three-Penny Memories, A Poetic Memoir
by Barbara Harris Leonhard

ISBN: 9781739757762

"Do you love your mother?" This provocative question provides the catalyst for this stunning poetic memoir from Pushcart Nominee Barbara Harris Leonhard. Through her artfully crafted poetry, the author considers where her love and loyalties lie following her ageing mother's diagnosis with Alzheimer's.

www.ingramcontent.com/pod-product-compliance
Lightning Source LLC
Chambersburg PA
CBHW071324080526
44587CB00018B/3343